NATIONAL GEOGRAPHIC

What Has Changed?

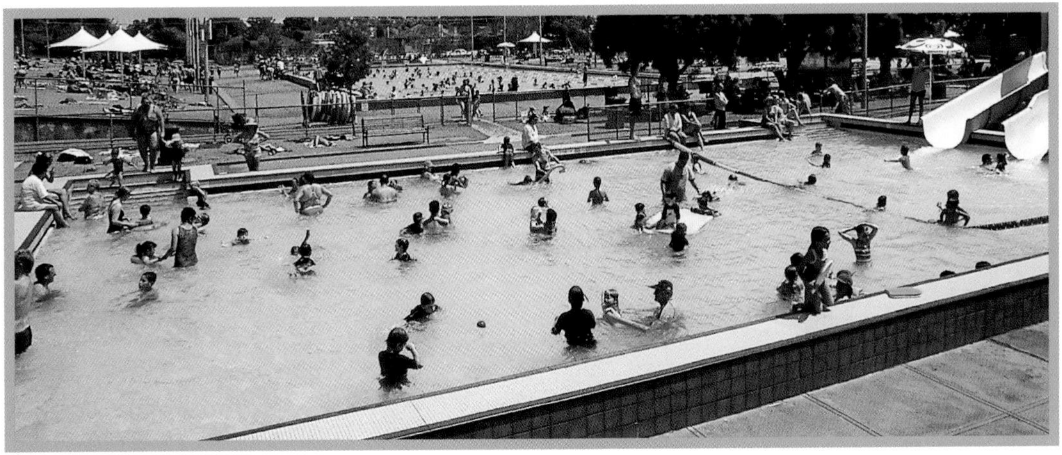

Karl Jensen

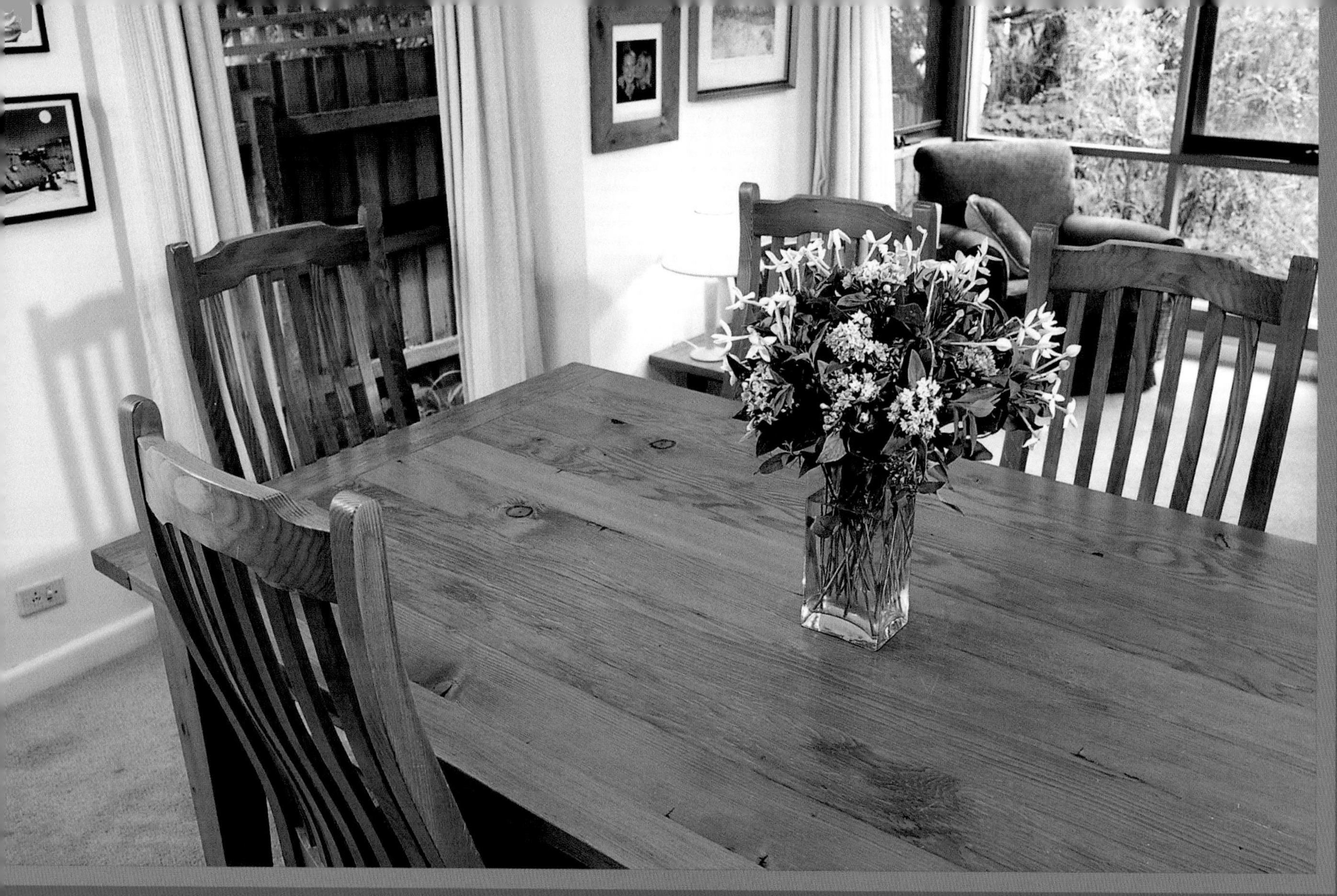

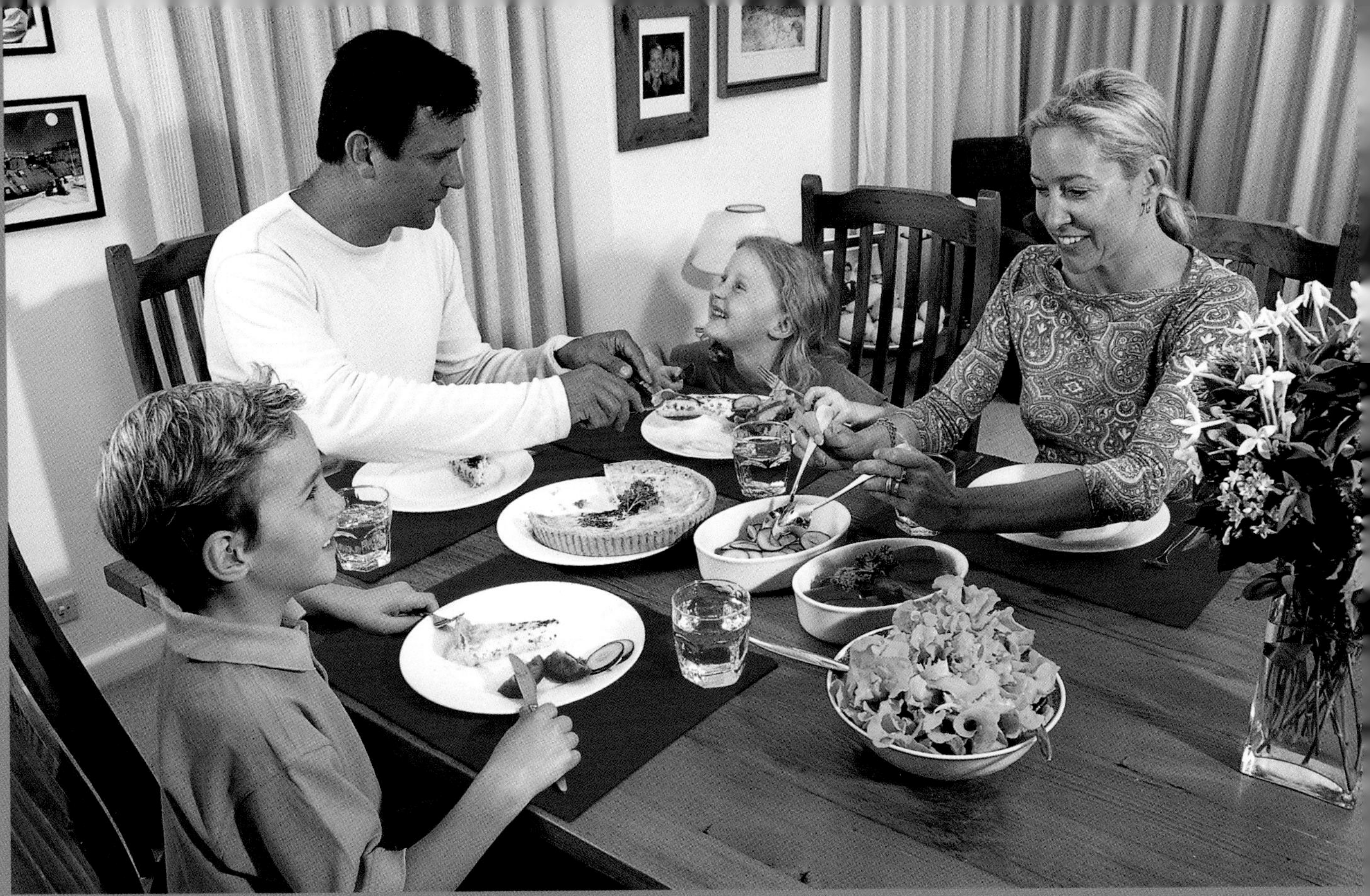

What has changed?

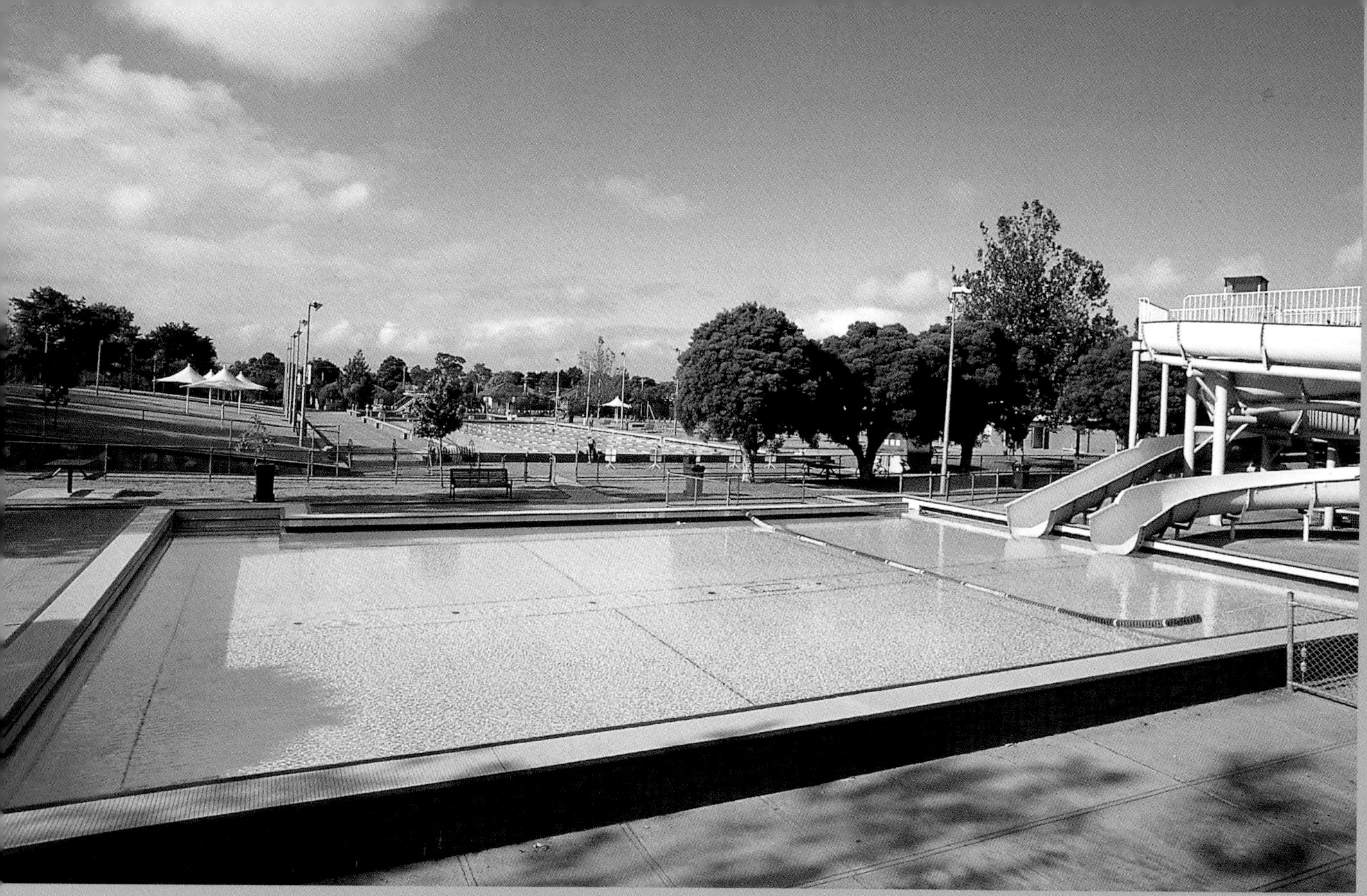

4

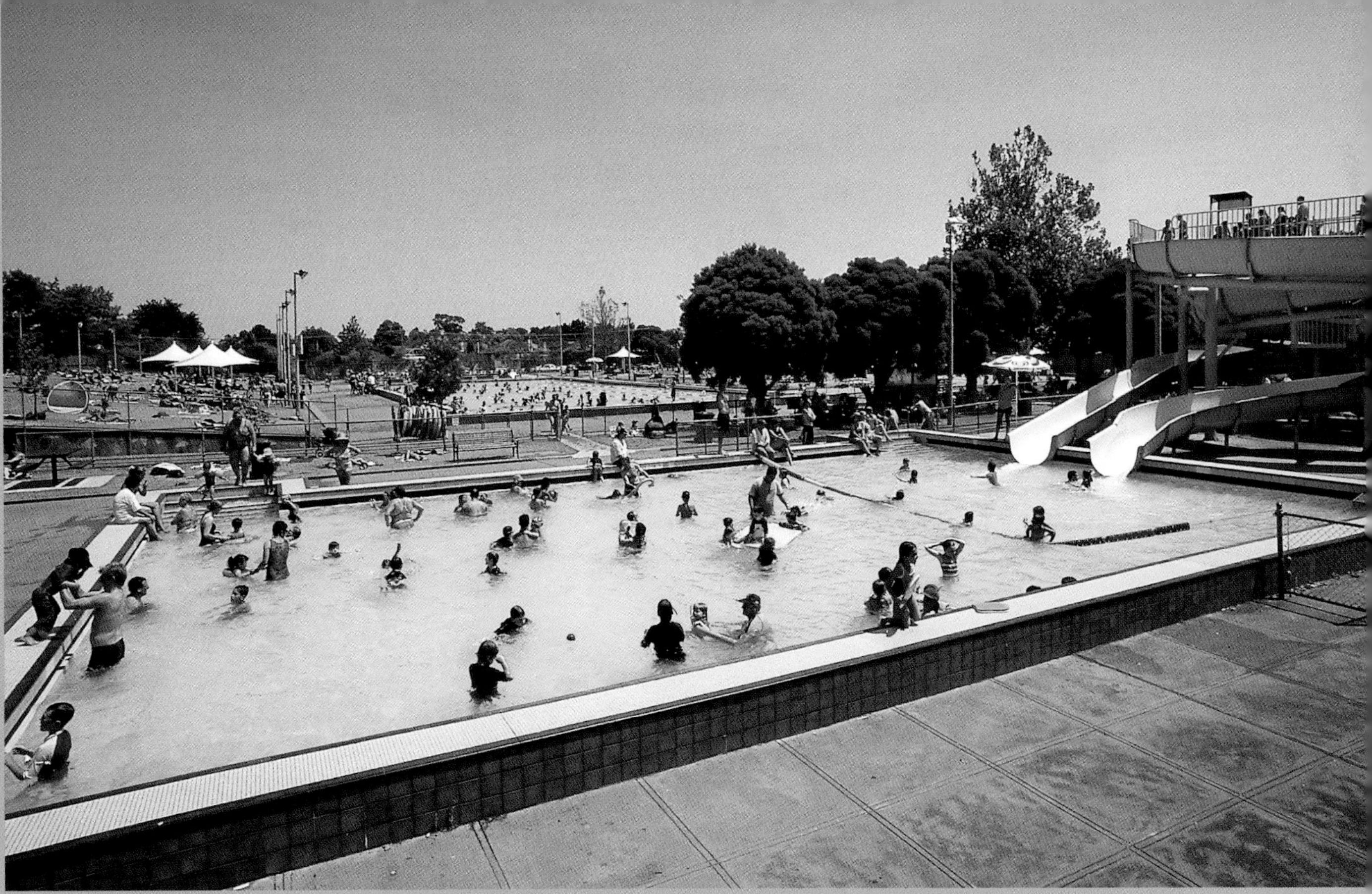

What has changed?

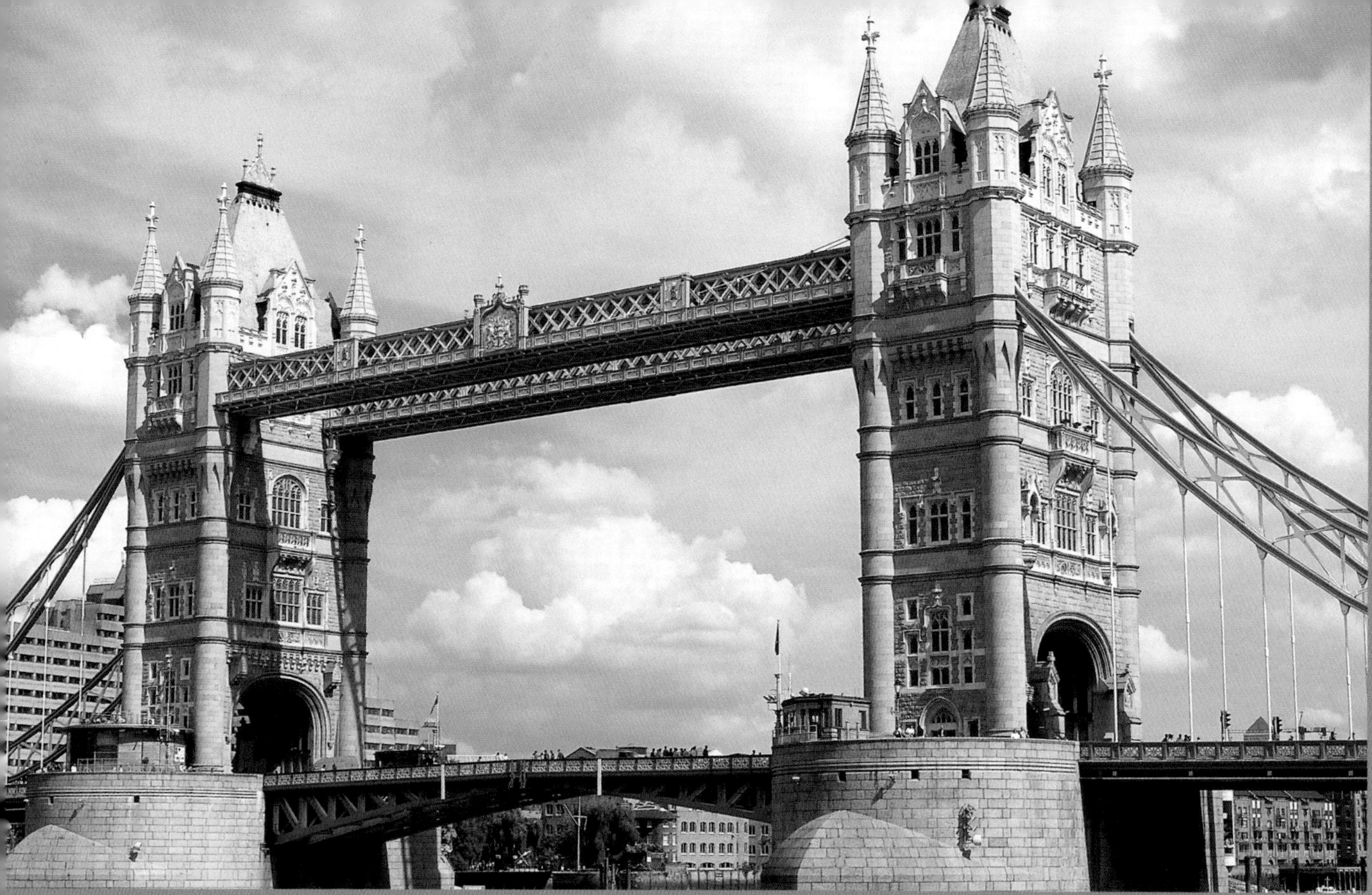

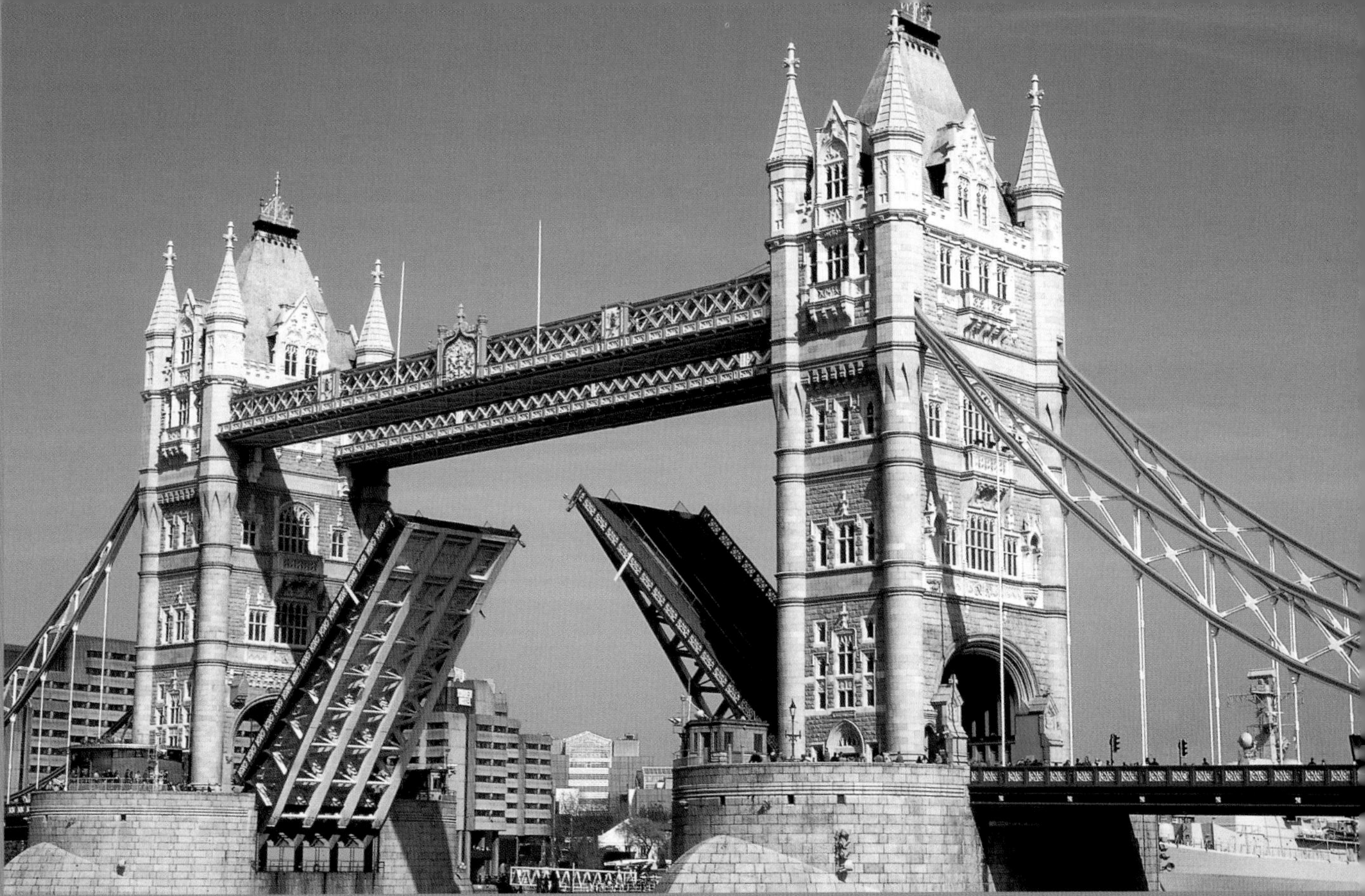

What has changed?

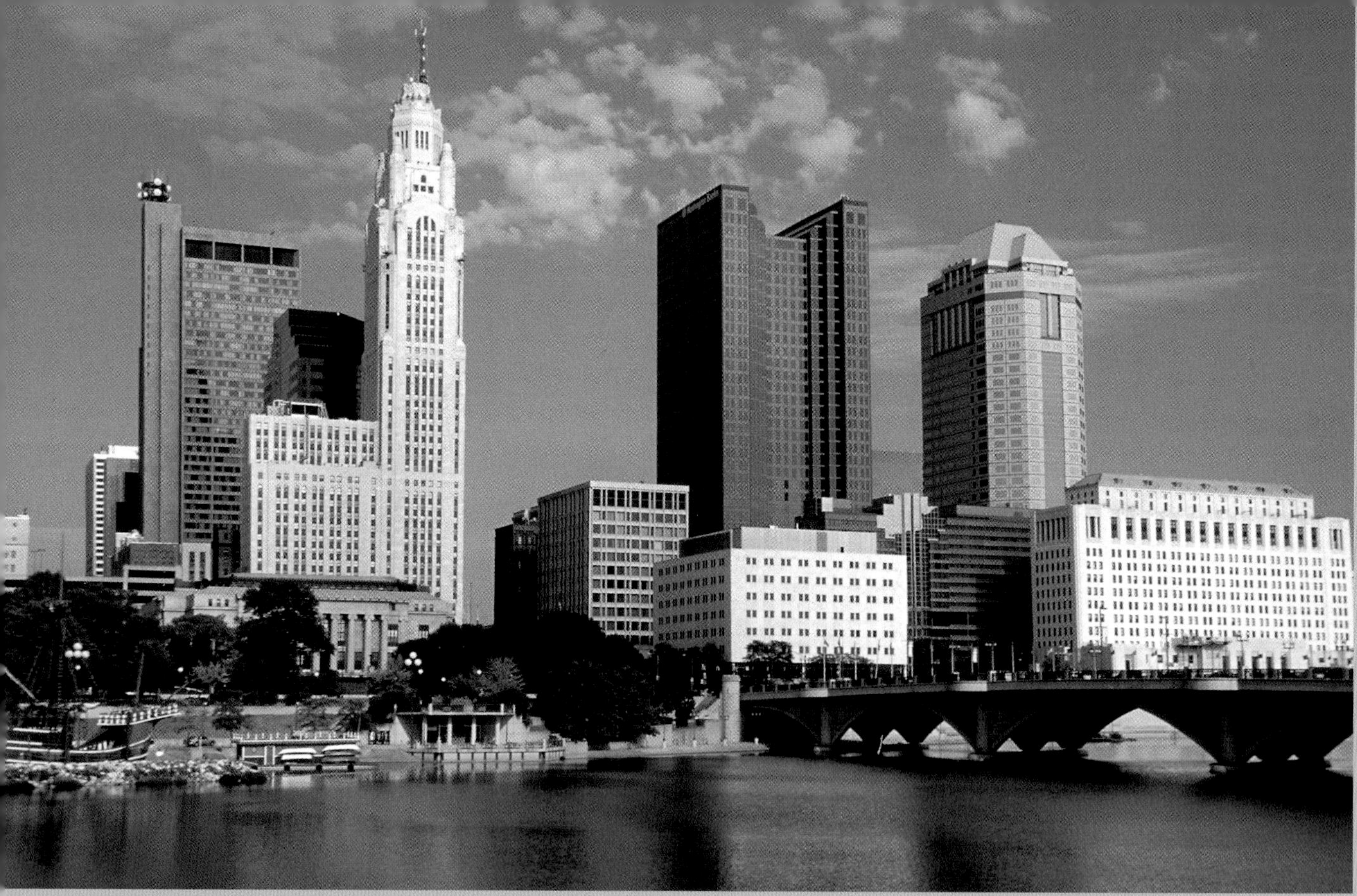

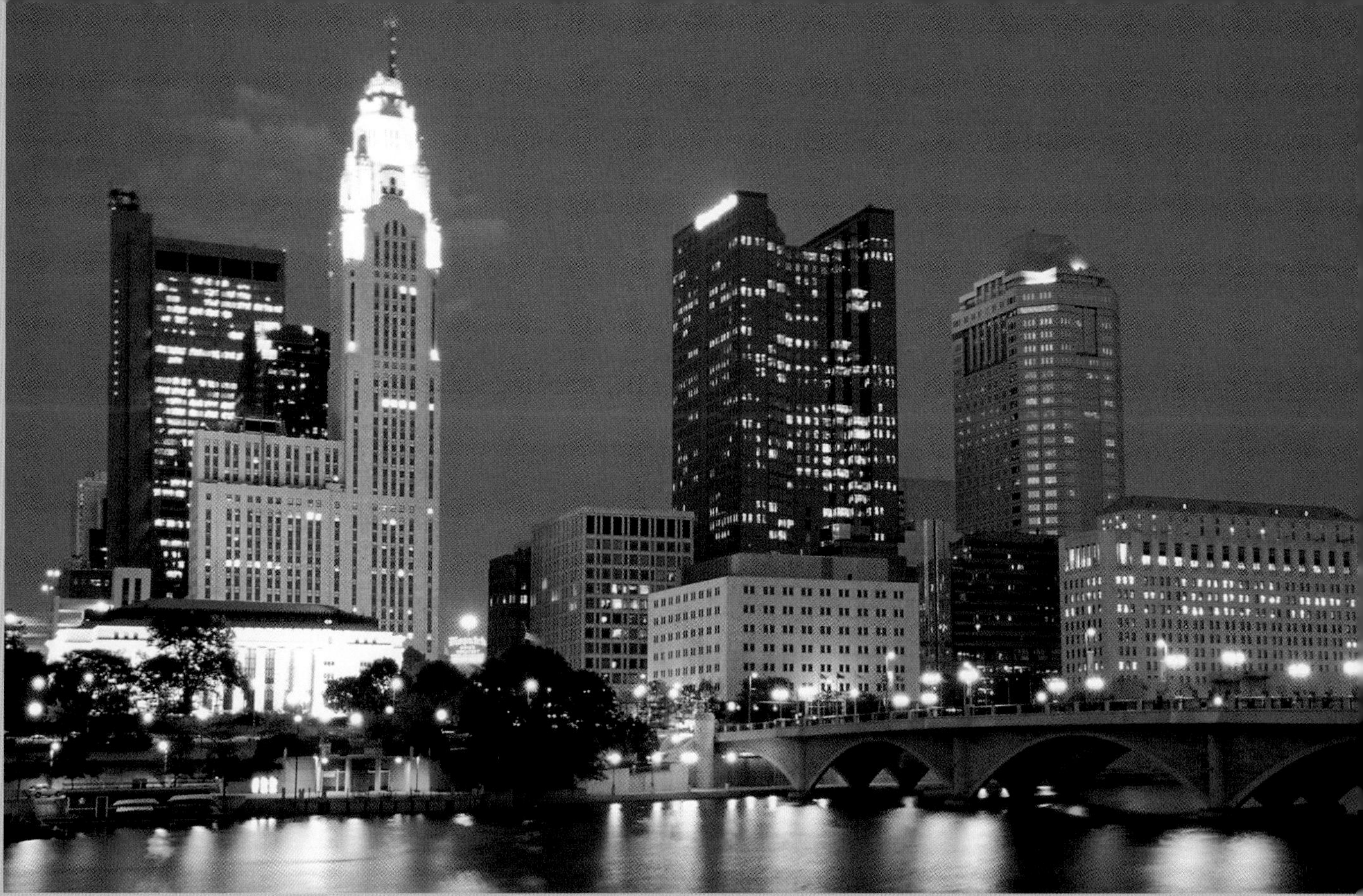

What has changed?

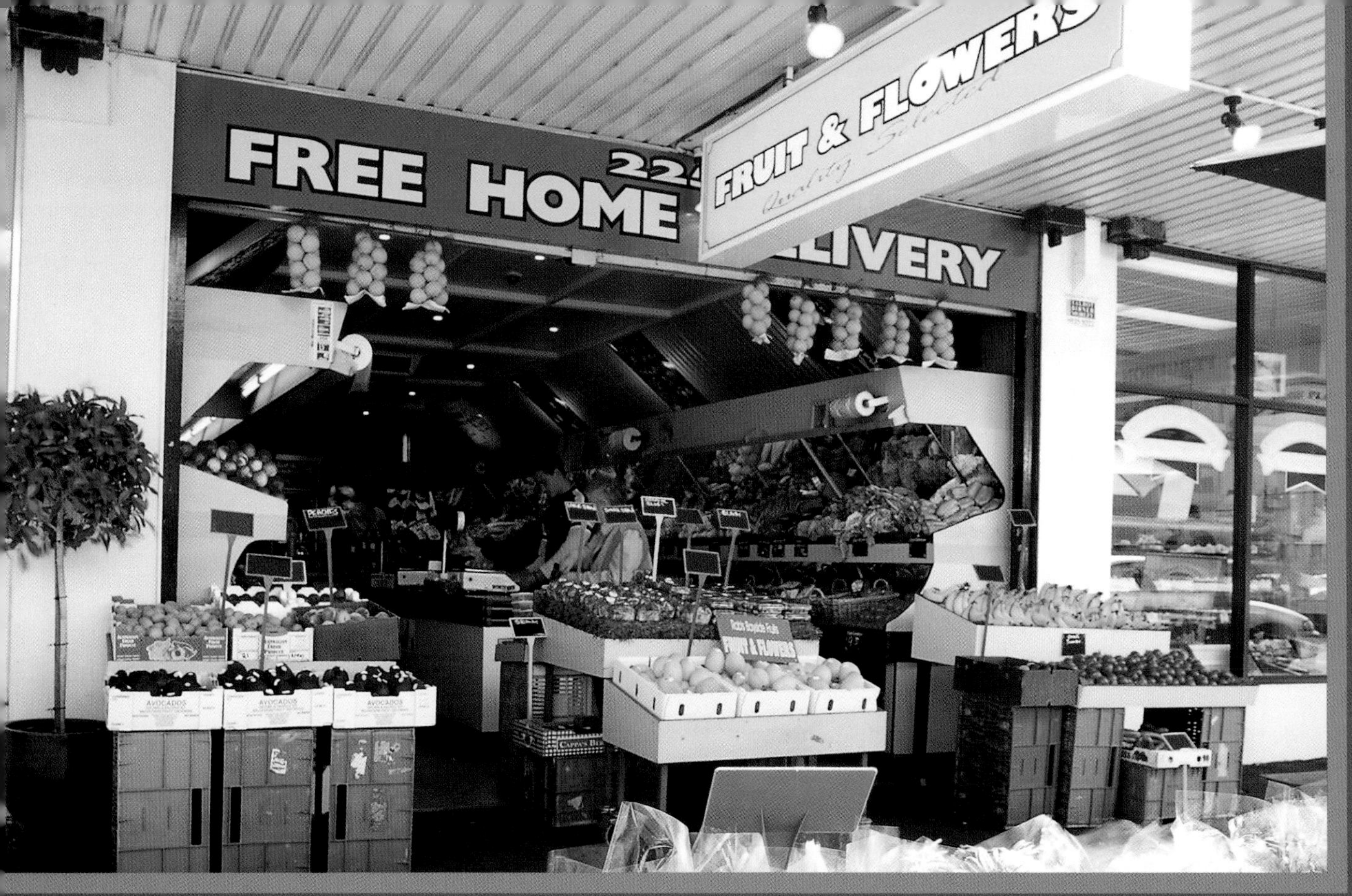
FREE HOME
LIVERY
FRUIT & FLOWERS
Quality Selected
AVOCADOS
FRUIT & FLOWERS

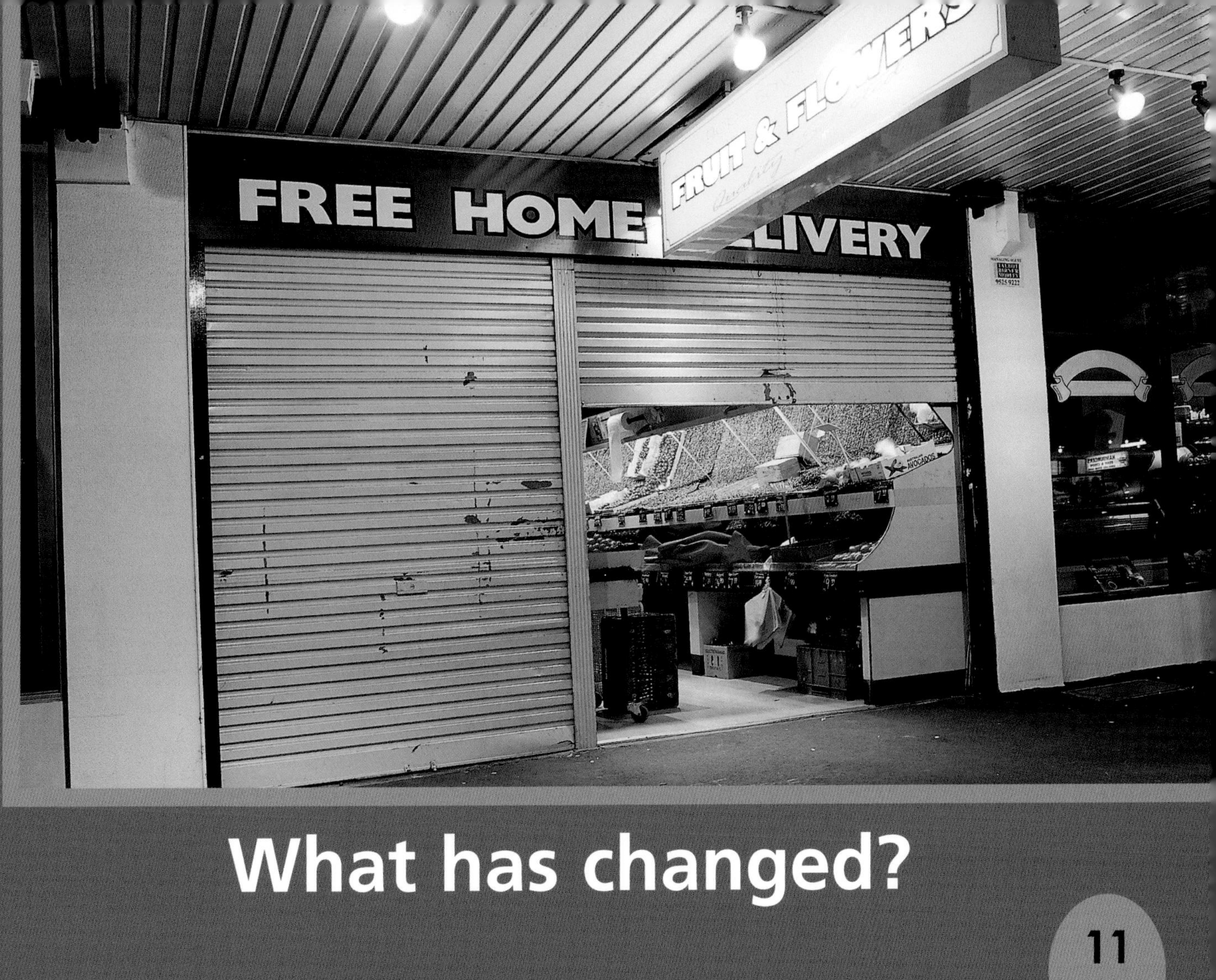

What has changed?

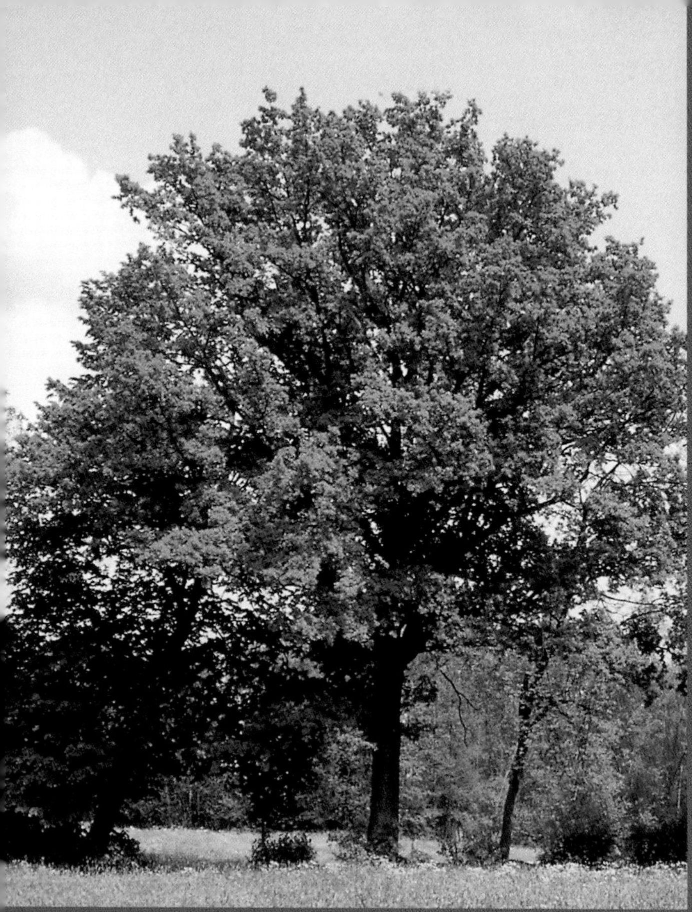

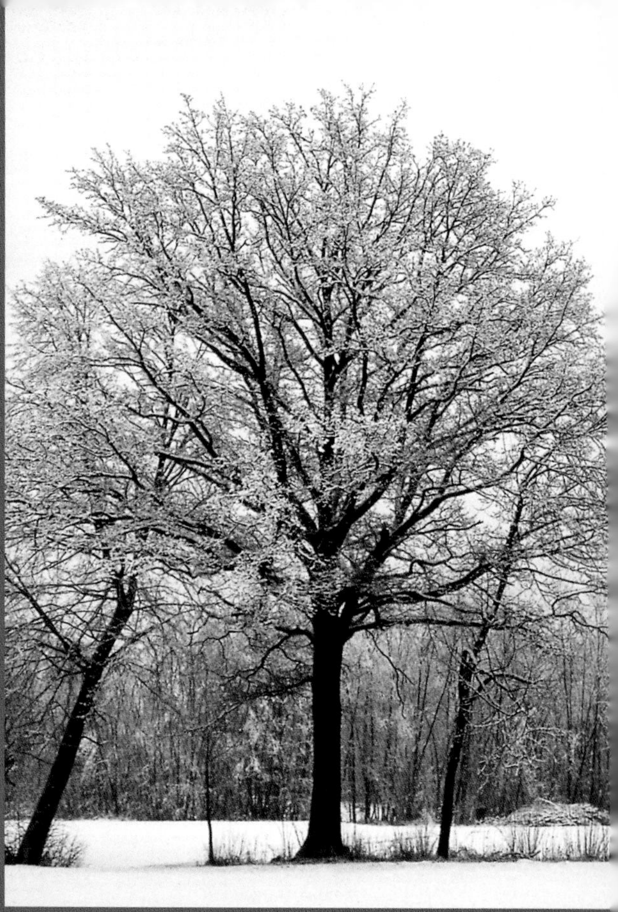

What has changed?